# 7 HOME BUYING SECRETS

*What Every Home Buyer Needs to Know*
*to Gain an "Unfair" Advantage*

**Aaron Wiens**

*Co-Founder of Wiens & Roth Real Estate*

★★★★★

"Wiens & Roth was recommended to us by trusted friends of ours, and we were extremely impressed with our initial meeting with them before we even began house searching. We knew nothing about the home-buying process (first-time home buyers here!), and he was very intentional with educating and training us to make sure we had the knowledge we needed to take this next step. We've been blown away by his team and the time and care they've dedicated to helping us find our home. We've loved working with this company, and we feel confident in recommending Wiens & Roth to anyone looking to buy or sell in the area!"

-Julie

★★★★★

"Incredibly helpful and supportive team, both from the selling side and buying side. We got superior guidance on the best strategy for putting in an offer that will be accepted. In addition, we sold our home with them, and got the Best-looking marketing (along with excellent advice and strategy) that you'll find in the region. Recommend 💯! Thank you!"

-Cami & Steve

# FORWARD

This is usually the part of a book where the author tells you about their HUGE business, including big statistics on why they are going to take over the world. In my opinion, you'll never remember those stats and odd claims. But you might remember this: I believe we genuinely care about our clients as people more than any other real estate company. Transactions are secondary. That is what makes us different.

Yes, we have a better chance at making you more money when you sell a home (due to our larger ad spend directly for you), and we know another 7 secrets than the ones listed below that help home buyers land their dream home, but what I hope you will remember is how we actually cared about you which is too uncommon in this industry. We don't hire our team members based on their sales volume or their polished pitches. In fact, most of our first team members had zero sales background or real estate training. BUT they cared about people.

I hope you enjoy this brief book and if you find anything in it worthwhile, can you do me two favors?

1) Follow us on social media.

2) Give this book to a friend who might benefit too.

If you want to learn more about us or contact us, visit wiensandroth.com. We'd love to hear from you!

P.S. I did not include my mother's 5 star review of our company in the testimonial page. If you want to get a laugh, visit our Wiens & Roth Facebook page to read her review. Thank goodness for mothers.

# CONTENTS

# PREFACE

Our company goal has always been to provide our buyer clients as much education as we possibly can. We believe that if we can take all the facts, all the experience, all the knowledge that we have acquired over the years AND download it to our buyer clients, they will be able to accomplish two things:

1) Have a comfort level with understanding the market, including why homes are priced the way they are, what to look for, and ultimately make the best decision on which home to purchase

2) Give them an advantage against the overwhelmingly uneducated buyers they are competing with. That is not to say the other buyers are uneducated, rather they are typically not nearly as prepared and armed with as much knowledge as our buyer clients are.

Word of warning. This book is derived from the many sit-downs we have had with buyers over the years. It will be terribly conversational, and less formal than my father would prefer his son to write for his first book. As a literature major, I am sure I am letting him down already. You're welcome, dad. There will be a ton of incorrect punctuation, incomplete sentences, and a ton of grammatical errors. Like this!?!

Disclaimer: This book is based on our experiences in Michigan and Ohio and may not completely relate to other markets. I am not an attorney or accountant, and this should not be construed as legal or tax advice.

# CHAPTER 1
# HOW TO MASTER TIMELINES

Timelines are life and death in a contract. The old saying, "Time kills all deals," couldn't be more true. If you want to master the process from writing a contract to getting the keys to your dream home, you need to be a master of timelines. Here we go!

There are three major timelines that are commonly accepted:

- Inspection contingency
- Financing contingency
- Closing drop dead date

Each of these timelines typically happen simultaneously and scaffold up to the closing date. Most of these dates are going to be fixed against a set point in the purchase agreement. We prefer to use the date when both buyer and seller sign the contract. We call this date "Acceptance".

Although each contract is different, for most buyers with a conventional loan, we prefer to use the following:

1. Inspection Contingency: 7-10 days
2. Financing Contingency: 30-40 days
3. Closing Date: approx 5 days after Financing Contingency

Let's (using a contraction already is going to take years off my dad's life) roleplay. We've just toured ten homes together and because of our "Homebuyer 101" over coffee, where you've learned to price per square feet, property taxes, special assessments, and we've made an accepted offer on the home we want...what are the next steps?

Step 1A) Make earnest deposit (more on that later)
Step1B) Meet with your lender to sign loan application.
Step 1C) Call to schedule inspection.
These are not step 1,2, and 3.

They are all the first step and need to be done ASAP so you can control and master the timeline! I know, I know. You're thinking that I am haggling over semantics. I can't stress how important it is to jump on (all of) step 1 right away, because it may come back to haunt you if there are any hiccups on the contingencies and everyday matters. Do hiccups in real estate happen? Haha. Yeah. Ever hear of COVID-19?

Why is mastering these timelines so important? A buyer needs to think of an accepted contract as a type of control of the property they want. Now imagine a scenario where another buyer wants the property badly and is offering more money to the seller. Do you think the seller is watching to see if those timelines are missed? Is it in the seller's best interest to provide an extension to those timelines or let the date slide if they can gain thousands of dollars more? Now you see.

## HOME *BUYER* SECRET #1:

Use number of days, not hard dates for timelines when able.

### *What do you mean?

Use X days from Acceptance. Do not use a date like March 11th.

## HOME *SELLER* SECRET #1:

Use hard dates, not number of days for timelines when able. Duh.

Too many times, a buyer has negotiated a deal with a hard date for one of their contingencies, and a seller has been slow, intentional or not, to sign the contract. It is a terrible bad practice to tell a buyer to start spending money on the typical inspection and financing costs when the seller hasn't signed the contract yet. One day turns into two days quickly, and now the buyer no longer has a 7-10-day window to conduct an inspection and they now have 5-8 days. Holidays, traveling, and inspector schedules tighten that window up quickly too. Let's say you have 8 days left for the inspection contingency and the inspector you want can only get there on day 7. Who has more leverage when you ask for repairs with less than a day to make a decision...you or the seller??

# CHAPTER 2
# WHAT IS AN EARNEST DEPOSIT?

Most buyers have no clue what an earnest deposit (EMD) is and how it works. In all fairness, they shouldn't, and it is our job to educate on what it is and how it is used. Lucky insider you! An earnest deposit is an amount of money you are required to deposit per purchase agreement terms. Here is what we teach about an earnest deposit: **It is your promise to the seller that you will close on the home no matter what.**

Common questions you might include:

1. How much should the deposit be?
2. Who do I write the check to?
3. Does it have to be a certified check?
4. Do I get it back?
5. Is it a fee or is it applied somehow?

Let's go over each of these.

Imagine a seller is comparing two similar offers where the only difference is that one offer has an earnest deposit of $500 and the other competing offer has an earnest deposit of $3,000.

Most sellers would rightfully suppose that the offer with the highest earnest deposit is the stronger offer put forth by a stronger buyer and thus more likely that the buyer will close on the home.

## HOME *BUYER* SECRET #2:

Use the earnest deposit as a weapon.

## HOME *SELLER* SECRET #2:

Use the earnest deposit as a weapon.

The earnest deposit is a negotiated amount and commonly found between a couple hundred dollars up to a certain percentage of the home's value. There really isn't a standard. If you are a savvy buyer that has been educated to know market values and what red flags to look for in a home, you can use the earnest deposit as a weapon. Most smart sellers understand terms are just as important as a high selling price and a buyer that is in a bidding war against other buyers might get away with not having the highest offer if they provide better terms. One of those terms is the earnest deposit.

We strongly advise using a third-party company like a title company to hold the earnest deposit. I believe it is a bad practice to allow the listing agent's company, the seller, or even the seller's attorney to hold the deposit. We recommend using using a title company to hold it 99.99% of the time. Typically, earnest deposits are under $10,000 and you can make a personal check written to the title company directly. Above $10,000, and a title company will probably want to see it wired.

In consideration to a seller, they have accepted your offer over the other offers, removed the property from the market, and aged the listing with days on the market so it looks stale if the buyer backs out. They are probably not happy if they have to start all over at this point. If they feel the buyer has not operated in good faith, the seller will feel hurt. It is our experience that sellers who feel hurt, want to hurt back and that can be via the earnest deposit.

Before our buyer clients write an offer, we want them to have the mindset that they will not receive their earnest deposit back if they do not close on the home. Although most of the time we are successful at negotiating language for it to be returned if a contingency is not met, there are only 3 ways to get a seller to release it:

1. Seller gives written permission to title company.
2. Court gives written directive to title company.
3. Title company follows the contract language and returns it

Please note that under the last instance, title companies are trying to be the non-partial 3rd party and very hesitant to make anyone upset and may request both parties to sign an agreement even when the contract says it is not required.

Unless the contract specifies or the court directs it, the seller doesn't get the earnest deposit. If there is no directive, the EMD would sit in the title company account until state law requires it to be released back to the buyer after a certain number of years.

One of the most common questions I receive is how the earnest deposit is applied or if it is just a lost fee. Prior to closing, you will receive a statement from the lender or title company that has a breakdown of all the costs, credits, and debits as well as who gets them. Where we operate, the earnest deposit is shown as a credit to the buyer and applied against the funds they would need to bring to closing. Essentially, if your earnest deposit is $500 then your down payment is $500 less.

# CHAPTER 3
# DON'T HIRE "CHUCK IN A TRUCK" TO INSPECT

9 9% of the time, we recommend our buyer clients to get a home inspection. The only possible exception to this is if they want to save money and forego hiring a home inspector on a newly construction home. Even then, I would still recommend a home inspection.

Here are the most common questions buyers have when it comes to inspection:

- Who should we hire?
- I have a friend that does electrical work, and he knows a lot about other things, can we hire him?
- How much does the inspection cost?
- Should I be at the inspection?
- What should we be looking for?

Let's dive in. I recommend a state-certified home inspector that provides pictures and a digital report. The reason you do not want to have a friend or family member do it for you is because we need to have an unbiased 3rd party create the report so that you have a better chance of having the seller remediate the issue. No one is going to trust your friend Jimmy the plumber when he says there is 2.5 years left on the roof.

The typical cost to a home inspection starts at around $300 (currently) for a base service. From there, the sky's the limit to add ons. I.e., radon testing, thermal imaging cameras, pest inspection, mold testing, etc.

We recommend that our buyer clients make themselves available to be there during the inspection process so that they can ask the inspector issues as they come up. It is a great way to gauge how serious an issue is or what some of the most common repairs can be.

Keep in mind, every home will have some type of defect(s). There is a difference between health and safety defects versus general wear and tear defects. Drywall cracks and creaking floorboards are common. We will let the home inspection experts determine if that is a sign of a major home settling issue or simply due to seasonal expansion and contraction. It has been our experience that anytime there has been major defects, the seller generally had no knowledge.

## HOME *BUYER* SECRET #3:

Share the inspection report with the seller on major health/safety issues to increase your odds of getting it fixed.

## HOME *SELLER* SECRET #3:

Use hard dates, not number of days for timelines when able.

Most good home sellers know that if there is a major issue, they probably need to fix it in order to sell the house and not look the other way. By providing the part of the home inspection with them on a major issue, you are essentially burdening them with an obligation to act on the new facts one way or another. They might as well come to a mutual agreement on the issue with your participation and feedback on the matter.

Please, please, please do not wait until the last minute to schedule an inspection. If you have a 10-day inspection period, you are better off having the inspection completed on day 2 than day 10. Imagine a scenario where you just beat out 5 other offers for the house of your dreams. The inspection report just came back with one *potentially* negative issue. If you completed the inspection early, you would then have plenty of time to further research it or have a second opinion on the potential severity of that issue. If you don't master the timeline and allow yourself to get jammed on or near the last day of your inspection contingency, do not expect the seller to have much sympathy and extend the inspection contingency for you.

Remember, a smart seller probably is working the other deals in case you miss your contingency deadline. You might be out of your earnest deposit, out of your loan application fees, and out of your inspector cost, AND you just lost the house of your dreams because you didn't have enough time to further examine the *potential* inspection issue.

There are three choices a buyer has when the inspection report comes back.

Choice 1) Move forward in purchasing the home as-is.
Choice 2) Give seller notice that you are terminating the contract due to a failed inspection
Choice 3) Ask the seller to consider making repairs, reducing the price, or providing a cash incentive to keep the deal moving forward

Each situation is unique, and each seller has a different motivation to sell. Has the home been on the market forever? Is it an estate sale? Were there multiple offers on the property? If you don't close on the home, will you be homeless at the end of the month? Each of those scenarios will determine the correct way to navigate the inspection contingency.

# CHAPTER 4
# CONVINCING A BANK TO GIVE YOU A BIG CHECK

The house just passed through inspection with no issues. Now what?? Now you are in the worst part of the deal...because you have to wait. And wait. Remember when you gave your lender every financial document you have ever had in your possession along with your driver's license, tax forms, paystubs, 9th grade student ID, etc?

The lender has been putting that info together in a package for the bank to get comfortable. Along with the appraisal (we'll get to that in a bit), all your financials get sent to an underwriter who has the responsibility to verify it is conforming to the loan standards. Once the underwriter gives their approval, you will get what is called "the clear to close".

We are going to back track to the appraisal. Do I believe an appraisal will give a value on what a home is worth? Nope. Do I believe that is a process for a bank to protect its investment? Bingo.

Cash offers do not need an appraisal. All other loans typically require an appraisal. More often than not, the appraisal value is going to come in pretty darn close to the purchase contract value. Magical! If there was not a contract, two appraisers might come up with massive differences in a home's estimated value. It is terribly subjective, and we have seen homes with seven offers and an appraiser will say the home is worth $10,000 less than the LOWEST of the 7 offers in their opinion. We have also seen the opposite in that an appraisal comes in hundreds of thousands of dollars more than the market value of a home, and a seller is frustrated that the appraisal number is unattainable. Maybe they should sell it to the appraiser. With all that said, I believe an appraisal is generally a good part of the process.

In the instance that the home you are purchasing does not meet the appraisal price, you have 3 options.

Choice 1) Move forward in purchasing the home as-is, with the knowledge that you will probably have to bring extra cash to closing in the difference of the purchase price and appraisal price.

Choice 2) Give seller notice that you are terminating the contract due to a failed financing contingency unless the seller reduces the purchase price to the appraised value. The bank will not lend you the money on the purchase contract price, only the appraised value.

Choice 3) Ask the seller to consider meeting you somewhere in the middle on a reduced price to keep the deal moving forward. You will still need to bring additional cash to closing.

Choice 4) See if your lender will let you order a second appraisal to be considered, or at a minimum contest the appraisal value.

If you have a VA loan, FHA loan, or USDA loan, there are more requirements that come up in the appraisal and I would talk to your agent on the specifics as it can be a little tricky if those loan programs require repairs.

## HOME *BUYER* SECRET #4:

If the home does not appraise for the contract purchase price, share the appraisal with the seller to increase your odds of a price reduction.

## HOME *SELLER* SECRET #4:

You have more leverage here than you believe as the buyer has already spent a considerable amount of money and might walk away with nothing to show for it. At the same time, you might not want them to walk away.

Assuming the appraisal came back fine on value, the underwriter will typically issue their "conditions of approval" or "conditions to close". Sometimes they need 10 items cleared up. Sometimes they don't need any. Common conditions include waiting for your employer to call back to verify employment or requesting an additional previous year tax return. Sometimes it can be more challenging, like asking an employer to renew your work contract early (for those on an employment contract). Sometimes it can be as easy as the scan of the driver's license was blurry, and they need a re-scan. In most instances, if you are this far into the process, a good lender is probably confident the loan will get approved.

As you are near the end of this financing contingency, this is a good time to set up the transfer of utilities for the day you are set to close or take possession.

# CHAPTER 5
# CLOSING COSTS

Before we get more in-depth on the Closing, it is so important that you understand what closing costs are and how they will ruin your day if you do not understand them.

No matter if you buy a house from a relative or a complete stranger, there will be closing costs. Even if you bring a suitcase of cash to the closing table, there will still be closing costs, albeit a little less.

Simply put, closing costs are fees and prepaids/escrows that a buyer AND a seller incur to transfer real estate confidently. There are typically three parts to closing costs:

1. lender fees
2. title fees
3. prepaids or escrows

We'll cover each one.

If buyers use an estimate of 2% to 3% of the value of the home, they will be pretty close. A $200,000 home should be about $5,000 +/- in typical closing costs. THIS IS NOT THE SAME AS A DOWN PAYMENT. A seller's closing costs are typically in the 7% to 8% range.

I used the word "confidently" in a previous paragraph because part of the closing costs for both a buyer and seller is the cost of title insurance. Incorrectly, many people think a title company is the only way to transfer property. The truth is, about anyone can transfer a deed and record it at the courthouse. You are probably wondering, "Why use a title company at all?" Title companies do quite a few things and doing the paperwork to transfer the property is just one of the functions. The primary reason for using a title company is for title insurance, and a large portion of the closing costs. Title insurance for a buyer is insurance against anyone claiming that the property is theirs. For example, let's say you just purchased the property from an estate and two brothers were the ones handling the house for their deceased parents. Low and behold, a month later, as you are cutting your grass in front of your new house, a lady comes up to you and says that it is her house and that her brothers (who thought their sister died in Africa on a mission trip but was really a secret CIA agent who went deep undercover to overthrow a drug lord) had no legal right to sell the home to you. Title insurance is a one-time payment at closing that the title company has looked at all the records and rights of ownership and they feel confident that clear title can be transferred to you and are willing to insure the property against other claims.

Another portion of your closing costs are lender fees. Most lenders charge an "origination fee", "processing fee", and/or "underwriting fee" which are common. A typical add-on for lenders is a fee called "points" which are a pre-payment for a reduced rate.

The last part of your closing costs are prepaids and escrows. This is not a true cost or a fee. Most lenders (and borrowers for that matter), want to see a consistent monthly payment AND know that the real estate taxes and home insurance is being paid. To do this, they will collect a certain amount above your principal and interest (P&I) payment that will cover both your real estate taxes and insurance. Most people consider that total amount their mortgage payment. The reason the lender does that is because the real estate taxing jurisdiction does not receive monthly payments, but usually bills two times a year. Depending on when you close on your home, the lender wants the real estate tax escrow account full so that it can pay the tax bill on time and gradually replenish that account evenly for the next time the tax bill is due. That part of the closing cost is actually partially funding your property taxes.

Home insurance is usually paid up front and part of your monthly mortgage payment is set aside in the escrow account for the next bill so it can be paid in full.

## HOME *BUYER* SECRET #5:

Buyers prefer to save their cash and have a Seller pay the Buyer's closing costs.

## HOME *SELLER* SECRET #5:

Sometimes this can affect an appraisal and a buyer that is willing to pay their own closing costs is usually considered a stronger buyer and resulting offer.

Well of course! But make no mistake, sellers are smart and know that if they are paying a buyer's closing costs, that the offer is effectively lower.

It has been our experience that our buyers prefer to pay a little higher monthly mortgage payment in order to bring less cash to the closing table. In general, they would rather have a larger rainy-day fund set aside for emergencies than to have a few thousand more in home equity. That is a personal decision, and it varies for every client.

Now let's do some quick math regarding an offer and closing costs. A home has an asking price of $200,000 and you want to make an offer. Part of your offer is to ask the seller to pay $5,000 of your closing costs. If you write them an offer of

$200,000.00 with $5,000 back toward closing costs, what is the seller actually receiving as their net offer? $195,000.

In another scenario, let's say you just toured the home and as you were leaving, you saw a family pull up to the house and they were going to tour the home next. In your mind, you made the decision that you want to put a strong offer in that night and hopefully before the family that toured after you puts in an offer. Your offer might look like $205,000 with $5,000 back toward buyer closing costs so that the seller feels like they are getting their full asking price.

# CHAPTER 6
# CLOSING ON THE HOME

Once you receive the "clear to close" from the lender signaling the loan is approved, the closing will be scheduled with the title company. If you were paying close attention to the section about timelines, you probably noticed that the deadline to close was later than the deadline for the financing contingency. Why is that? After the financial meltdown and recession circa 2008, there is a provision in the Dodd-Frank legislation that requires 3 "rest days" between full loan approval and the closing date. Business days, NOT calendar days. For example, if you need 40 days after Acceptance for financing contingency, we would typically then write a closing deadline of 45 days after Acceptance. Let's say you received a clear to close on Friday. The soonest you could close would be the following Wed.

When the lender gives full loan approval, they also put together a Closing Disclosure or "CD". This will outline the actual down payment, interest rate, how much the bank is calculating for property taxes and insurance, etc. You are required to sign this document before closing.

What then happens behind the scenes is that the title company is getting the loan funds from your lender as well as setting up the payoff (if there is a mortgage in place) for the seller's mortgage as well as putting together the files both the buyer and seller need to sign for the loan, state documents, and other documents to transfer the property.

You are probably wondering what to expect when you show up to the title company to close. When all goes according to plan, you will sign a large stack of documents and your hand will be tired after signing your life away. This should take about 20 minutes when it all goes smoothly.

In many instances, the seller (roundtable closing) will be in the same room and they will sign their documents too, but with much less paperwork. 9 times out of 10, it is a very amicable and pleasant experience talking with the seller as you are both happy. In most instances, you will also get the KEYS to the home too! When it is a seller's market, you may have given them extra time in the house after closing in order to make your offer more appealing. In that case, there will probably be a discussion about how we will handle a transfer of the keys in the coming weeks.

Believe it or not, our team gets mixed emotions at closing. We are extremely happy that our clients have landed the house they wanted, but we also know that the time we have regularly carved out of our week to show you homes (and getting to know you more) has ended. In some ways, it's like the playground friend graduated. It's no coincidence we spend a lot of money and time in putting together a personal closing gift for all our buyer clients/friends. You better invite us to the housewarming party! BTW, we bring great housewarming gifts so if that is not a good enough reason to invite us, I don't know what is.

# CHAPTER 7
# WHAT TO LOOK FOR IN A HOME OR WHY WE LIKE A GRANDMA HOUSE FOR FIRST TIME HOME BUYERS

Most first-time home buyers have a budget that prevents them from buying something from Architectural Digest. Some type of compromise is going to be needed on location or updates.

Although the "updates" you see on flips, and the decorating and color schemes look great in the pictures on the listing websites, that doesn't necessarily mean it is a great home to buy. Those features draw buyers in, and as our buyers are touring the home, we are looking at un-sexy features: are the windows original or replaced, what condition and age is the furnace, does the roof look newer or tired, is the hot water tank near the end of its expected life, are there PEX plumbing lines or copper, etc. We are not inspectors, and this is not an inspection. However, those items are all mental checkmarks in compiling a pro-con list of what makes a responsible home purchase. You need to be looking at these items too. If every item is in good condition, but the hot water tank is way past needing replacement, does that mean you should not buy the house? Maybe, but all things considered, the hot water tank is one of the least expensive items and it sounds like the home has more positive items in the pro-con ledger than negative items.

Do you know what most first-time buyers hate? The "grandma house" with ugly paint colors, weird smells, and old shag carpet. Most first-time home buyers watch HGTV and see beautiful finishes and updates everywhere and are trained to buy that type of house.

Do you know what the most inexpensive updates you can do to a house to add value are? Paint and replace carpet.

Here is the thing about a "grandma house"...when there was something important that needed fixing, grandma would have it done. And it would be done the right way. If the furnace needed repair a couple of times, grandma would have it replaced. If a few windows were needed replacing, grandma would replace all of them at once. If the roof had a leak, grandma wouldn't add another roof layer. She would do a complete tear off and start new.

Sure, her kitchen cabinets are dated and look older. But grandma waxed those every Saturday morning and cared for them because she remembered what it was like during the

Great Depression. Change the hardware on those cabinets and it will make a big difference.

## HOME *BUYER* SECRET #6:

Look for a "grandma house".

## HOME *SELLER* SECRET #6:

If you are selling a "grandma house" you might want to have it repainted and recarpeted. You might get more buyers to take a look at it.

We like "grandma homes" for our first-time home buyers. You should start liking them if this is your first house on a budget.

We have plenty of red flags though. Each of these is not a deal killer on its own but be careful as these can add up to big expenses. Here are the top 5 red flags:

1. **Dated electrical**. This can be a large undertaking to update BY A PROFESSIONAL. This falls under safety and health red flags.

2. **Wet basement or crawl**. 9/10 homes have had water in the basement due to either a broken sump pump or gutter downspouts not extended. Those are easy fixes and not as big of a concern if fixed and remediated quickly and properly. Anything else can be a big-ticket issue and a huge red flag.

3. **Structural/foundation issues**. It may show up as water in the basement as mentioned above. Drywall cracks are common and do not necessarily mean there is a structural issue. However, anything that looks out of place in the basement or crawl should be noted and have a professional look at it.

4. **Roof leaks**. There should not be an active roof leak and the problems will literally trickle down from that. Just avoid unless you are a roofer.

5. **The lipstick flip**. This is a home that a buyer bought cheap and put inexpensive coverings over dated areas. Lick and stick backsplash, contractor grade carpeting, Menard's clearance light fixtures, and peel-adhesive faux tile flooring. This makes us nervous as a heart attack because we are concerned that instead of fixing something the right way, they are passing the issue on to a sucker buyer. It is the things we can't see behind the flip lipstick that makes us wonder if the home is really a smelly pig.

If your budget allows you to spend more, we can offer this general advice without having to know your preferences or circumstances: **try to buy the most inexpensive home in a nice neighborhood**. The nicest neighborhoods are better at retaining value. This is the most risk-averse way to purchase.

# CHAPTER 8
# HOME BUYING STRATEGIES

Whatever you do, I strongly advise against writing an offer with the pre-meditated strategy of reducing the offer after the inspection no matter what. That is a recipe for disaster. Here is an example: There are several offers for a $200,000 home. You want to pay $190,000 for the home. You try to win the bidding with a $210,000 offer. The inspection report shows normal wear and tear for a home that age and condition. You then ask the seller for $20,000 off the purchase price because the roof is not new (even though the current roof has no issues, and you know that). What do you think a seller is going to do? That "strategy" will typically cost you the inspection fee, probably the loan application fee, maybe the appraisal fee. And you just might have a little fight on your hands over the earnest deposit with a seller who feels you did not proceed in good faith.

There are legitimate reasons to reduce the purchase price after an inspection, but don't set yourself up for failure using that as a pre-meditated strategy.

I would classify our buyers into having a personality of one of these two groups:

Group 1) The buyer who knows what they want and are ready to write an offer the day a property comes to the market. They generally consider themselves as quick decision makers and are ready to buy a home without the need for drawn out negotiation.

Group 2) The buyer who may want to tour a home two to four times before concluding the home is right for them. They would feel comfortable not purchasing a home than overpaying $500 more than they think it is worth.

We honestly don't prefer buyers in one group or the other. The reason we need to characterize as to which group our buyer belongs to will completely relate to their expectation of what is a good outcome *for them*!

Of course, in a seller's market, the second group generally has a difficult time responding quick enough and that's why this chapter is so important.

If you would identify more closely to the second group, here is the strategy that will benefit you the most.

1) Look for homes that have sat on the market for more than 30 days. If the seller has been that patient to not have sold yet, you will have time on your side to think and negotiate.

2) Identify homes that have really unpopular features that you do not mind. The more unique the house is, the smaller the pool of buyers you are competing against.

3) Think about "pocket areas" that are on the edge of your target neighborhoods. Because the home is not on the exact street that every buyer wants, that house might not get the same competitive buyer activity and that can work in your favor.

4) Don't lowball the offer but balance it between price and terms so that the seller will still be able to give you a counteroffer to keep the conversation going.

If you would identify as being in the first group, you are probably better suited for a better outcome in a seller's market. There are still some obstacles we want to prepare you for though. Here is the strategy to help.

1) Know the market price per square foot. That way, when you walk into a home, you feel confident if the home is overpriced or underpriced.

2) This will sound strange, but ignore the asking price. If we have done our job of educating you on the market, and you feel confident in pricing homes, you will be better prepared to compete for a home. For example: If on the first day on the market of a home there are 5 offers and you know it is underpriced by $20,000, then you are at an advantage over other buyers.

3) Especially in a competitive seller market, you might need to ask yourself the question, "at what price am I okay with another buyer getting the home", regardless of the asking price. That might be your best and final offer.

## HOME *BUYER* SECRET #7:

The key to a great offer isn't a lowball or asking price offer. Both may not get accepted depending on what you are competing against. Sometimes you are competing against other buyers, other times you is competing against the seller's patience. The key in any market is to make the offer just good enough that a seller will have to think twice about even countering the offer and risk losing it. That gray area is where you can shave a few thousand dollars off the bottom line and win.

## HOME *SELLER* SECRET #7:

Don't be caught up with just a final purchase price number. Great terms can be just as valuable than cash. And if you have a good offer, you might want to think twice and take the bird in hand.

## SUMMARY

Here are the home buying secrets (and seller secrets) all in one place for quick reference:

### HOME *BUYER* SECRET #1:

Use number of days, not hard dates for timelines when able

### HOME *BUYER* SECRET #2:

Use the earnest deposit as a weapon.

### HOME *BUYER* SECRET #3:

Share the inspection report with the seller on major health/safety issues to increase your odds of getting it fixed.

### HOME *BUYER* SECRET #4:

If the home does not appraise, share the appraisal with the seller to increase your odds of a price reduction.

### HOME *BUYER* SECRET #5:

Buyers prefer to save their cash and have a Seller pay the Buyer's closing costs.

### HOME *BUYER* SECRET #6:

Look for a "grandma house".

## HOME *BUYER* SECRET #7:

The key to a great offer isn't a lowball or asking price offer. Both may not get accepted depending on what you are competing against. Sometimes you are competing against other buyers, other times it is the seller's patience. The key in any market is to make the offer just good enough that a seller will have to think twice about even countering the offer at risk they may lose it. That gray area is where you can shave a few thousand dollars off the bottom line and win.

And because you made it this far, I am going to share a bonus secret that might be the most important one.

## BONUS HOME *BUYER* SECRET:

The number one rule in real estate is to never have to purchase a home right when you need to. Be patient and opportunistic.

# HOME *SELLER* SECRETS SUMMARY

## HOME *SELLER* SECRET #1:

Use hard dates, not number of days for timelines when able.

## HOME *SELLER* SECRET #2:

Use the earnest deposit as a weapon.

## HOME *SELLER* SECRET #3:

Use hard dates, not number of days for timelines when able.

## HOME *SELLER* SECRET #4:

You have more leverage here than you believe as the buyer has already spent a considerable amount of money and might walk away with nothing to show for it. At the same time, you might not want them to walk away.

## HOME *SELLER* SECRET #5:

Sometimes this can affect an appraisal and a buyer that is willing to pay their own closing costs is usually considered a stronger buyer and resulting offer.

## HOME *SELLER* SECRET #6:

If you are selling a "grandma house" you might want to have it repainted and recarpeted. You might get more buyers to take a look at it.

## HOME *SELLER* SECRET #7:

Don't be caught up with just a final purchase price number. Great terms can be just as valuable than cash. And if you have a good offer, you might want to think twice and take the bird in hand.

## BONUS HOME *SELLER* SECRET:

The number two rule in real estate is to never have to sell a home right when you need to. Don't trap yourself into a fire sale. Duh.

Happy Hunting.

Made in the USA
Monee, IL
26 October 2021